LifeExcellence

TREASURY OF QUOTES

Edited by
Brian E. Bartes

LEGACY PUBLISHING GROUP
Plymouth, Michigan

www.treasuryofquotes.com

Published in Plymouth, Michigan, by Legacy Publishing Group, P.O. Box 700424, Plymouth, MI 48170.

www.treasuryofquotes.com

Design by 1106 Design, Phoenix, Arizona

Publisher's Cataloging-in-Publication
(Provided by Quality Books, Inc.)

LifeExcellence treasury of quotes / edited by Brian E.
  Bartes.
    p. cm.
    ISBN-13: 978-0-9776773-1-3
    ISBN-10: 0-9776773-1-1

    1. Quotations. I. Bartes, Brian E. II. Title:
  Life Excellence treasury of quotes.

PN6081.L54 2010   082
                    QBI10-600112

To Heidi, for always believing in me.

Introduction

The wisdom of the wise and the experience
of the ages are perpetuated by quotations.
— BENJAMIN DISRAELI

The quotations, when engraved upon the memory,
give you good thoughts. They also make you
anxious to read the authors and look for more.
— WINSTON CHURCHILL

I quote others only to better understand myself.
— MICHEL DE MONTAIGNE

For as long as I can remember, I have been
motivated and inspired by quotes. Still today, I
can't help but to write down, cut out, or copy
quotes that stand out as being important advice
on how to live my life. Quotes are powerful, and
the wisdom they provide has made a profound
impact on my life.

The very best quotes contain simple words and
phrases that cause the reader to reflect deeply,

and ultimately move him or her to do something.
They are an inspiration, and a call to action.

Why this anthology? My collection of quotes,
though better organized than ever, still includes
several envelopes containing small bits of
paper—some handwritten, some typed, and
many clipped from newspapers or magazines.
I have wanted for some time to distill this
collection down to the quotes that have meant
the most to me personally.

The collection of quotes contained in this book
has inspired me to create excellence in every
area of my life. These quotes have motivated me
to positively impact life around me, hopefully in
a way that has made a difference in the world.
It is my great hope that they will have that effect
on you, too.

—Brian Bartes

LifeExcellence

TREASURY OF QUOTES

To accomplish great things,
we must not only act,
but also dream; not only
plan but also believe.

ANATOLE FRANCE

If you can imagine it, you
can achieve it; if you can
dream it, you can become it.

WILLIAM ARTHUR WARD

Cherish your visions and
your dreams, as they are
the children of your soul;
the blueprints of your
ultimate achievements.

NAPOLEON HILL

All our dreams can come true, if we have the courage to pursue them.

WALT DISNEY

Dreams come a size too big so that we can grow into them.

JOSIE BISSET

The future belongs to
those who believe in the
beauty of their dreams.

ELEANOR ROOSEVELT

At first, dreams seem
impossible, then improbable,
and eventually inevitable.

CHRISTOPHER REEVE

The only place where your dream becomes impossible is in your own thinking.

ROBERT H. SCHULLER

Nothing happens unless first a dream.

CARL SANDBURG

The only way to discover
the limits of the possible
is to go beyond them
into the impossible.

ARTHUR C. CLARKE

Whether you believe
you can do a thing or
not, you are right.

HENRY FORD

There is nothing like a
dream to create the future.

VICTOR HUGO

When you want something,
all the universe conspires in
helping you to achieve it.

PAULO COELHO

Vision without action is merely a dream. Action without vision just passes the time. Vision with action can change the world.

JOEL BARKER

Vision is the art of seeing things invisible.

JONATHON SWIFT

Perpetual optimism is
a force multiplier.

COLIN POWELL

What we see
depends mainly on
what we look for.

SIR JOHN LUBBOCK

The only thing that stands between a man and what he wants from life is often merely the will to try it and the faith to believe that it is possible.

RICHARD M. DEVOS

I dwell in possibility.

EMILY DICKINSON

If we all did the things
we are capable of doing,
we would literally
astound ourselves.

THOMAS EDISON

People become really quite
remarkable when they start
thinking that they can do
things. When they believe
in themselves they have
the first secret of success.

NORMAN VINCENT PEALE

The quality of a person's
life is in direct proportion
to their commitment to
excellence, regardless of their
chosen field of endeavor.

VINCE LOMBARDI

Excellence is the
gradual result of always
striving to do better.

PAT RILEY

We are what we repeatedly
do. Excellence then, is
not an act, but a habit.

ARISTOTLE

The future belongs to the competent: resolve to join the top 10% of people in your field and your future will be unlimited.

BRIAN TRACY

Don't judge each day by the harvest you reap, but by the seeds you plant.

ROBERT LOUIS STEVENSON

The discipline of personal mastery starts with clarifying the things that really matter to us and living our lives in the service of our highest aspirations.

PETER M. SENGE

What lies behind us and
what lies before us are
tiny matters compared
to what lies within us.

RALPH WALDO EMERSON

To affect the quality
of the day, that is the
highest of arts.

HENRY DAVID THOREAU

Twenty years from now you will be more disappointed by the things you didn't do than by the ones you did do. So throw off the bowlines. Sail away from the safe harbor. Catch the trade winds in your sails. Explore. Dream. Discover.

MARK TWAIN

The best way to predict
the future is to create it.

PETER DRUCKER

Learn how to be happy with
all that you have while you
pursue all that you want.

JIM ROHN

Enjoy the little things,
for one day you may look
back and realize they
were the big things.

ROBERT BRAULT

The best things in
life aren't things.

ART BUCHWALD

How different our lives are when we really know what is deeply important to us and, keeping that picture in mind, we manage ourselves each day to be and to do what really matters most.

STEPHEN R. COVEY

Things which matter most
must never be at the mercy
of things which matter least.

JOHANN WOLFGANG
VON GOETHE

We make a living by what
we get, but we make a
life by what we give.

WINSTON CHURCHILL

We must not, in trying to think about how we can make a big difference, ignore the small daily differences we can make which, over time, add up to big differences that we often cannot foresee.

MARIAN WRIGHT EDELMAN

Make a commitment
today to something bigger
and more important
than yourself.

BRIAN TRACY

The greatest use of life is
to spend it for something
that will outlast it.

WILLIAM JAMES

Destiny is not a matter of chance, it is a matter of choice; it is not a thing to be waited for, it is a thing to be achieved.

WILLIAM JENNINGS BRYAN

Life is not measured by the number of breaths we take, but by the moments that take our breath away.

MAYA ANGELOU

You ought to be afraid
to die until you've
contributed something
great back to humanity.

Oliver Wendell Holmes

Life isn't a matter of
milestones, but of moments.

Rose Kennedy

Life is a song—sing it.
Life is a game—play it.
Life is a challenge—meet it.
Life is a dream—realize it.
Life is a sacrifice—offer it.
Life is love—enjoy it.

SAI BABA

See each morning as if it were the morning of the very first day. Treasure each day as if it were the evening of the very last day.

AUTHOR UNKNOWN

Each happiness of yesterday is a memory for tomorrow.

GEORGE WEBSTER DOUGLAS

You must live in the present, launch yourself on every wave, find your eternity in each moment. Fools stand on their island opportunities and look toward another land. There is no other land; there is no other life but this.

HENRY DAVID THOREAU

Start with modest goals,
and then find a great team
to work with…. It takes
only a few great people
to turn modest goals
into something big.

JOHN SCULLEY

The tragedy of life doesn't
lie in not reaching your
goal. The tragedy lies in
having no goal to reach.

BENJAMIN E. MAYES

Never doubt that a small group of committed citizens can change the world. Indeed, it is the only thing that ever has.

MARGARET MEAD

There is only one corner
of the universe you can
be certain of improving
and that's your own self.

ALDOUS HUXLEY

Set your goals high, and
don't stop till you get there.

BO JACKSON

Life is either a daring adventure or nothing.

HELEN KELLER

The ultimate reason for setting goals is to entice you to become the person it takes to achieve them.

Jim Rohn

Setting a goal is not the main thing. It is deciding how you will go about achieving it and staying with that plan.

Tom Landry

As long as you're
going to be thinking
anyway, THINK BIG.

DONALD TRUMP

Hitch your wagon to a star.

RALPH WALDO EMERSON

Imagine no limitations;
decide what's right and
desirable before you
decide what's possible.

BRIAN TRACY

If you are lucky enough
to find a way of life you
love, you have to find
the courage to live it.

JOHN IRVING

When you follow your bliss... doors will open where you would not have thought there would be doors; and where there wouldn't be a door for anyone else.

JOSEPH CAMPBELL

Learn to listen. Opportunity
could be knocking at
your door very softly.

FRANK TYGER

Let yourself be silently
drawn by the strange pull
of what you really love.
It will not lead you astray.

RUMI

Use what talents you possess; the woods would be very silent if no birds sang except those that sang best.

HENRY VAN DYKE

Hold yourself responsible
for a higher standard than
anybody expects of you.

HENRY WARD BEECHER

The difference between a
successful person and others
is not a lack of strength,
not a lack of knowledge,
but rather a lack of will.

VINCE LOMBARDI

The difference between the impossible and the possible lies in a man's determination.

TOMMY LASORDA

It's kind of fun to do the impossible.

WALT DISNEY

The best time to plant a tree was 20 years ago. The second best time is *now*.

CHINESE PROVERB

There are two mistakes one can make along the road to truth—not going all the way, and not starting.

BUDDHA

He that would have the
fruit must climb the tree.

THOMAS FULLER

If we wait for the moment
when everything, absolutely
everything is ready, we
shall never begin.

IVAN TURGENEV

Even if you are on the right track, you will get run over if you just sit there.

WILL ROGERS

You don't have to be great to get started, but you have to get started to be great.

LES BROWN

If opportunity doesn't knock, build a door.

MILTON BERLE

Action may not always bring happiness; but there is no happiness without action.

BENJAMIN DISRAELI

Whatever you can do, or
dream you can do, begin it.
Boldness has genius,
power and magic in it.

JOHANN WOLFGANG
VON GOETHE

The great thing in this world is not so much where we stand as in what direction we are moving.

Oliver Wendell Holmes

Opportunities multiply
as they are seized.

SUN TZU

Everyone who got
where he is had to
begin where he was.

ROBERT LOUIS STEVENSON

All success is, really, is
having a predetermined
plan and carrying it
out successfully over a
long period of time.

HARVEY MACKAY

The road on the extra
mile is never crowded.

BRIAN BARTES

The best motivation is self-motivation. The guy says, "I wish someone would come by and turn me on." What if they don't show up? You've got to have a better plan for your life.

JIM ROHN

The path to success
is to take massive,
determined action.

ANTHONY ROBBINS

Just Do It.

NIKE SLOGAN

The people that get on in this world are the people that get up and look for the circumstances that they want; and if they can't find them, they make them.

GEORGE BERNARD SHAW

Every morning in Africa a gazelle wakes up. It knows it must run faster than the fastest lion or it will be killed. Every morning a lion wakes up. It knows it must outrun the slowest gazelle or it will starve to death. It doesn't matter whether you are a lion or a gazelle— when the sun comes up, you had better be running.

AUTHOR UNKNOWN

You can do anything if
you work and keep
on working; if you try
and keep on trying.

AUTHOR UNKNOWN

Talent is cheaper than
table salt. What separates
the talented individual
from the successful one
is a lot of hard work.

STEPHEN KING

You have to perform at
a consistently higher level
than others. That's the mark
of a true professional.

JOE PATERNO

Do your best every
day and your life will
gradually expand into
satisfying fullness.

HORATIO W. DRESSER

I'm a great believer in luck,
and I find the harder I work,
the more luck I have.

 THOMAS JEFFERSON

Genius is one percent
inspiration and ninety-
nine percent perspiration.

THOMAS EDISON

Continuous effort—not
strength or intelligence—
is the key to unlocking
our potential.

WINSTON CHURCHILL

Work like you don't need
the money. Love like you've
never been hurt. Dance
like nobody is watching.

MARK TWAIN

Deliver more than you are getting paid to do. The victory of success will be half won when you learn the secret of putting out more than is expected in all that you do.

OG MANDINO

Some people dream of success while others wake up and work hard at it.

AUTHOR UNKNOWN

You can become anything you want to be, as long as you believe in yourself and are willing to work hard enough to attain your goals.

BRIAN BARTES

The ultimate victory in competition is derived from the inner satisfaction of knowing that you have done your best and that you have gotten the most out of what you had to give.

HOWARD COSELL

Always bear in mind that your own resolution to succeed is more important than any other one thing.

ABRAHAM LINCOLN

It's a funny thing about life: If you refuse to accept anything but the best you very often get it.

SOMERSET MAUGHAM

You will never find time for anything. If you want time, you must make it.

CHARLES BUXTON

There is no scarcity of opportunity to make a living at what you love; there's only a scarcity of resolve to make it happen.

WAYNE DYER

Most of the important things in the world have been accomplished by people who have kept on trying when there seemed to be no hope at all.

DALE CARNEGIE

People of mediocre ability sometimes achieve outstanding success because they don't know when to quit. Most men succeed because they are determined to.

GEORGE E. ALLEN

It's not that people want too much; it's that they want too little.

AUTHOR UNKNOWN

Don't say you don't have enough time. You have exactly the same number of hours per day that were given to Helen Keller, Louis Pasteur, Michelangelo, Mother Teresa, Leonardo da Vinci, Thomas Jefferson and Albert Einstein.

H. JACKSON BROWN, JR.

Focus on where you want
to go, not on what you fear.

ANTHONY ROBBINS

Courage is resistance to
fear, mastery of fear—
not absence of fear.

MARK TWAIN

Our doubts are traitors,
and make us lose the
good we often might win,
by fearing to attempt.

WILLIAM SHAKESPEARE

If you listen to your fears,
you will die never knowing
what a great person you
might have been.

ROBERT H. SCHULLER

Our plans miscarry if they have no aim. When a man does not know what harbor he is making for, no wind is the right wind.

Seneca

Feel the fear and do it anyway.

Susan Jeffers

A ship in a harbor is safe, but that is not what ships are built for.

WILLIAM SHEDD

Only those who risk going too far can possibly find out how far they can go.

T. S. ELIOT

This nation was built by men who took risks; pioneers who were not afraid of the wilderness, businessmen who were not afraid of failure, scientists who were not afraid of the truth, thinkers who were not afraid of progress, dreamers who were not afraid of action.

BROOKS ATKINSON

One does not discover new
lands without consenting
to lose sight of the shore
for a very long time.

ANDRÉ GIDE

Do not go where the
path may lead; go instead
where there is no path
and leave a trail.

RALPH WALDO EMERSON

Only those who dare
to fail greatly can ever
achieve greatly.

ROBERT F. KENNEDY

Failure is not the worst
thing in the world. The
very worst is not to try.

AUTHOR UNKNOWN

When you get into a tight place and everything goes against you till it seems as though you could not hold on a minute longer, never give up then, for that is just the place and time that the tide will turn.

HARRIET BEECHER STOWE

Many of life's failures are
people who did not realize
how close they were to
success when they gave up.

THOMAS EDISON

Obstacles don't have to
stop you. If you run into
a wall, don't turn around
and give up. Figure out
how to climb it, go through
it, or work around it.

MICHAEL JORDAN

If you want to increase
your success rate, double
your failure rate.

THOMAS WATSON, SR.

Every adversity, every
failure, every heartache
carries with it the seed of
an equal or greater benefit.

NAPOLEON HILL

Mistakes are the
portals of discovery.

JAMES JOYCE

Success is seldom achieved
by people who contemplate
the possibility of failure.

WILLIAM FEATHER

Nothing in this world can take the place of persistence. Talent will not; nothing is more common than unsuccessful men with talent. Genius will not; unrewarded genius is almost a proverb. Education will not; the world is full of educated derelicts. Persistence and determination alone are omnipotent.

CALVIN COOLIDGE

The greatest glory in living
lies not in never falling, but
in rising every time we fall.

NELSON MANDELA

Fall seven times,
stand up eight.

JAPANESE PROVERB

Obstacles are those
frightful things you see
when you take your
eyes off your goal.

HENRY FORD

Challenges can be stepping
stones or stumbling blocks.
It's just a matter of how
you view them.

AUTHOR UNKNOWN

Life is a grindstone.
But whether it grinds
us down or polishes us
up depends on us.

L. Thomas Holdcraft

The significant problems
we face today cannot be
solved at the same level
of thinking we were at
when we created them.

Albert Einstein

Winners never quit and
quitters never win.

VINCE LOMBARDI

I learned that if you want
to make it bad enough,
no matter how bad it
is, you can make it.

GALE SAYERS

We were born to
succeed, not to fail.

HENRY DAVID THOREAU

Perseverance,
n. A lowly virtue whereby
mediocrity achieves an
inglorious success.

AMBROSE BIERCE

The stars are constantly shining, but often we do not see them until the dark hours.

EARL RINEY

If we don't change our direction, we are likely to end up where we are going.

CHINESE PROVERB

Don't fear failure so much
that you refuse to try new
things. The saddest summary
of life contains three
descriptions: could have,
might have and should have.

LOUIS E. BOONE

I am not discouraged,
because every wrong
attempt discarded is
another step forward.

THOMAS EDISON

We must either find a
way or make one.

HANNIBAL

Man's mind, once stretched
by a new idea, never regains
its original dimensions.

OLIVER WENDELL HOLMES

Once you have decided
what you want, act as
if it were impossible to
fail, and it shall be!

DOROTHEA BRANDE

It's a little like wrestling
a gorilla. You don't quit
when you're tired—you quit
when the gorilla is tired.

ROBERT STRAUSS

A pessimist sees the
difficulty in every
opportunity; an optimist
sees the opportunity
in every difficulty.

WINSTON CHURCHILL

That which we persist in
doing becomes easier—not
that the nature of the task
has changed, but our ability
to do it has increased.

RALPH WALDO EMERSON

People do not fail;
they simply quit trying.

AUTHOR UNKNOWN

You miss 100% of the
shots you don't take.

WAYNE GRETZKY

Failure is the opportunity
to begin again more
intelligently.

HENRY FORD

The winners in life think
constantly in terms of I can,
I will, and I am. Losers, on
the other hand, concentrate
their waking thoughts on
what they should have
or would have done, or
what they can't do.

DENNIS WAITLEY

It is not the critic who counts: not the man who points out how the strong man stumbles or where the doer of deeds could have done better. The credit belongs to the man who is actually in the arena, whose face is marred by dust and sweat and blood, who strives valiantly, who errs and comes up short again and again, because there is no effort without error or shortcoming, but who knows the great enthusiasms, the great devotions, who spends himself for a worthy cause; who, at the best, knows, in the end, the triumph of high achievement, and who, at the worst, if he fails, at least he fails while daring greatly, so that his place shall never be with those cold and timid souls who knew neither victory nor defeat.

THEODORE ROOSEVELT

If we listened to our intellect, we'd never have a love affair. We'd never have a friendship. We'd never go into business, because we'd be cynical. Well, that's nonsense. You've got to jump off cliffs all the time and build your wings on the way down.

RAY BRADBURY

When one door closes another door opens; but we so often look so long and so regretfully upon the closed door, that we do not see the ones which open for us.

ALEXANDER GRAHAM BELL

What would you attempt
to do if you knew you
could not fail?

AUTHOR UNKNOWN

Do, or do not.
There is no try.

YODA

"Come to the edge,"
he said. They said,
"We are afraid."
"Come to the edge,"
he said. They came,
he pushed them,
and they flew.

GUILLAUME APOLLINAIRE

Treat people as if they were what they ought to be, and help them to become what they are capable of being.

JOHANN WOLFGANG
von GOETHE

They may forget what you said, but they will never forget how you made them feel.

CARL W. BUECHNER

Some people come into our
lives and quickly go. Others
stay for awhile and make
footprints on our hearts. And
we are never, ever the same.

AUTHOR UNKNOWN

No person can lead other
people except by showing
them a future. A leader
is a merchant of hope.

NAPOLEON BONAPARTE

Keep away from people who belittle your ambitions. Small people always do that, but the really great make you feel that you, too, can become great.

Mark Twain

People don't care how much you know, until they know how much you care.

Zig Ziglar

If you talk to your children, you can help them to keep their lives together. If you talk to them skillfully, you can help them to build future dreams.

JIM ROHN

It seems essential, in relationships and all tasks, that we concentrate only on what is most significant and important.

SØREN KIERKEGAARD

Never discourage anyone who continually makes progress, no matter how slow.

ARISTOTLE

Your attitude, not your aptitude, will determine your altitude.

ZIG ZIGLAR

Associate reverently, as much as you can, with your loftiest thoughts.

HENRY DAVID THOREAU

Ability is what you're capable of doing. Motivation determines what you do. Attitude determines how well you do it.

LOU HOLTZ

The way to love anything is to realize that it might be lost.

G. K. CHESTERTON

You can have everything
in life you want, if you
will just help enough other
people get what they want.

ZIG ZIGLAR

There comes that mysterious
meeting in life when
someone acknowledges
who we are and what we
can be, igniting the circuits
of our highest potential.

RUSTY BERKUS

To laugh often and much; to win the respect of intelligent people and the affection of children; to earn the appreciation of honest critics and endure the betrayal of false friends; to appreciate beauty, to find the best in others; to leave the world a little better; whether by a healthy child, a garden patch or a redeemed social condition; to know even one life has breathed easier because you have lived. This is the meaning of success.

RALPH WALDO EMERSON

If you will do what most people are not *willing* to do, you will accomplish what most people are not *able* to do.

BRIAN BARTES

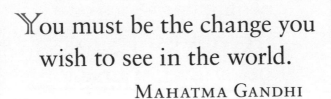

You must be the change you wish to see in the world.

MAHATMA GANDHI

The tragedy of life is not that it ends so soon, but that we wait so long to begin it.

W. M. Lewis

Don't bother just to be better than your contemporaries or predecessors. Try to be better than yourself.

William Faulkner

Everyone thinks of changing the world, but no one thinks of changing himself.

LEO TOLSTOY

It is never too late to become what you might have been.

GEORGE ELLIOT

A journey of a
thousand miles begins
with a single step.

<small>CHINESE PROVERB</small>

If you were starting over
today, what would you do
differently? Whatever your
answer, start doing it now.

<small>BRIAN TRACY</small>

To be what we are, and to become what we are capable of becoming, is the only end of life.

ROBERT LOUIS STEVENSON

The reward of a thing well done is to have done it.

RALPH WALDO EMERSON

Think of yourself as on the threshold of unparalleled success. A whole, clear, glorious life lies before you.

ANDREW CARNEGIE

We could all use a little coaching. When you're playing the game, it's hard to think of everything.

JIM ROHN

It's what you learn after
you know it all that counts.

JOHN WOODEN

Live as if you were to
die tomorrow. Learn as if
you were to live forever.

MAHATMA GANDHI

Don't wish it was easier;
wish you were better. Don't
wish for less problems;
wish for more skills. Don't
wish for less challenge;
wish for more wisdom.

JIM ROHN

Life is a journey, not
a destination.

AUTHOR UNKNOWN

Live your life each day as you would climb a mountain. An occasional glance toward the summit keeps the goal in mind, but many beautiful scenes are to be observed from each new vantage point. Climb slowly, steadily, enjoying each passing moment; and the view from the summit will serve as a fitting climax for the journey.

HAROLD V. MELCHERT

Life is a great big canvas,
and you should throw all
the paint on it you can.

DANNY KAYE

May you live every
day of your life.

JONATHAN SWIFT

Yesterday is history.
Tomorrow is a mystery.
And today? Today is
a gift. That's why we
call it The Present.

BABATUNDE OLATUNJI

Life is a succession of
moments. To live each
one is to succeed.

CORITA KENT

Far away, there in the sunshine, are my highest aspirations. I may not reach them, but I can look up and see their beauty, believe in them, and try to follow them.

LOUISA MAY ALCOTT

I have learned this at least by my experiment: that if one advances confidently in the direction of his dreams, and endeavors to live the life which he has imagined, he will meet with a success unexpected in common hours.

HENRY DAVID THOREAU